Pope Francis

MARIE MORREALE

Children's Press®
An Imprint of Scholastic Inc.

Content Consultant
Michael P. Murphy, PhD
Director, Catholic Studies
Loyola University
Chicago, Illinois

Library of Congress Cataloging-in-Publication Data
Names: Morreale, Marie, author.
Title: Pope Francis / Marie Morreale.
Description: New York : Childrens Press, 2016. | Series: A true book | Includes bibliographical
  references and index.
Identifiers: LCCN 2016008154| ISBN 9780531219737 (library binding) | ISBN 9780531221181 (pbk.)
Subjects: LCSH: Francis, Pope, 1936– —Juvenile literature. | Popes—Biography—Juvenile literature.
Classification: LCC BX1378.7 .M67 2016 | DDC 282.092—dc23
LC record available at http://lccn.loc.gov/2016008154

Front cover: Pope Francis with a
dove in St. Peter's Square
Back cover: Pope Francis with a child

Find the Truth!

Everything you are about to read is true *except* for one of the sentences on this page.

Which one is **TRUE**?

T or F   Pope Francis was born in Italy.

T or F   Pope Francis taught in schools for many years.

Find the answers in this book

Contents

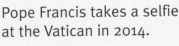

THE **BIG** TRUTH!

Pope Francis takes a selfie
at the Vatican in 2014.

Bergoglio riding public transportation

Vatican City

Jorge's grandparents and father had moved from Italy to Argentina.

Jorge Bergoglio was the oldest of five children in his family.

CHAPTER 1

The Boy Who Would Be Pope

On December 17, 1936, Jorge Mario Bergoglio was born to Mario and Regina Bergoglio in Flores, Argentina. Flores is a suburb of Buenos Aires, Argentina's capital and largest city. Mario worked as an accountant. Regina stayed at home to raise the children. Many relatives lived nearby. They had big family dinners and played soccer together. No one would have thought Jorge would become **Pope** Francis, head of the Catholic Church.

Family Life

Jorge was very close with his mother. She was a fabulous cook, and he loved to watch her make huge feasts. He liked helping her and learned some of her recipes. They would often listen to opera on the radio together. Jorge also enjoyed listening to his grandparents, parents, aunts, uncles, and cousins share stories of life back in Italy. He especially loved when his great uncle sang old Italian songs.

Jorge had a very close relationship with his parents (left).

Many people in Buenos Aires live in poverty.

The Bergoglios were very happy. But sometimes when they visited Buenos Aires, Jorge would see another side of life. Many of the people there were very poor. Some were homeless, some sick, and some children didn't go to school. The images of people begging for money or food, the rundown shacks, and the sad children sparked something in Jorge's heart. Even as a child, he knew he wanted to help those in need.

As a teenager, Jorge loved to learn. He read books, magazines, and newspapers. Jorge also loved science. He studied chemistry

in high school and later at technical school. He eventually worked in a laboratory. But he wasn't all work and no play. He supported his local soccer team, San Lorenzo de Almagro. He also loved dancing, especially the tango. His large circle of friends knew him as a fun guy.

Soccer and stamp collecting were among Jorge's childhood hobbies.

A New Calling

Jorge has said he realized he wanted to be a priest one night when he was out with friends. They passed a church, and Jorge went inside. He talked with a priest he had not met before. Though he recalls little of the conversation, Jorge remembers feeling suddenly and strongly that he should become a priest. He was 17 years old. When he was 20, he entered the **seminary** at Villa Devoto in Buenos Aires and studied **theology**.

Jorge lived in this room while studying to become a priest in Buenos Aires.

Finding His Path

Not long after he started at Villa Devoto, Bergoglio suffered a serious lung illness called pleurisy. Surgeons had to take out most of one of his lungs. Recovery was difficult and painful, but he soon returned to his studies.

In 1958, Bergoglio moved north to the city of Córdoba. There, he officially started his training as a **novice** with the Society of Jesus, also known as the Jesuits.

Córdoba is the second-largest city in Argentina.

Bergoglio, dressed in priest's garments, poses with his family.

There are many **orders**, or groups, a priest
can belong to in the Catholic Church. The Jesuit
order focuses on education, as well as charity and
spreading religious teachings. Jesuits also look
inward, at themselves. They work to become aware
of their own feelings and their relationship to God.
This practice informs a Jesuit's actions toward
himself and in support of the world at large.

As an ordained priest, Father Bergoglio preached during masses.

CHAPTER 2

The Journey to Rome

Bergoglio completed his training as a novice in 1960. He took the vows of poverty, loyalty, and obedience to the church that all Jesuits take. This made him an official member of the Jesuit order, but he still needed more training. During the next nine years, Bergoglio studied as a scholastic, or a Jesuit working toward priesthood. He also taught in Jesuit high schools. In 1969, Bergoglio was **ordained** a priest, making him Father Bergoglio.

A Born Teacher

Father Bergoglio loved teaching. He enjoyed showing young students the joy of reading. By the early 1970s, he was named novice master at the Jesuit seminary in San Miguel, Argentina. This placed him in charge of teaching the novices there. He also became the Jesuit provincial superior of Argentina, supervising all Jesuit activity in the country for a six-year term. This was a big honor.

Father Bergoglio (center) conducts a church service alongside his fellow Jesuits in San Miguel.

As he took on higher leadership positions, Father Bergoglio gave up most of his teaching duties. But he really missed sharing knowledge with students. In the 1980s, he returned to the classroom. He spent several

Father Bergoglio was a dedicated teacher.

years teaching at Jesuit colleges in Buenos Aires. He took time for his own studies, too, first in Ireland and later in Germany. His work also took him to Rome, Italy.

Even as Bergoglio rose through the ranks in the Catholic Church, he continued to take public transportation.

Changes

In 1990, Father Bergoglio's career took a major turn. Church officials pulled him from his duties because they thought his leadership was too rigid and controlling. They assigned him to Córdoba. The move was difficult, and Father Bergoglio was deeply unhappy. But it was also a time of growth and service. As he suffered, he could better relate to and help others who suffered.

Father Bergoglio spent nearly two years in Córdoba. He left in 1992 when he was made a bishop of Buenos Aires. This made him leader of all Catholics in a section of the city. Jesuits generally do not seek positions of such power, so the situation was unusual. It was even more unusual six years later when Father Bergoglio became archbishop, head of the Catholic Church in Buenos Aires. He was the first Jesuit to hold this position.

As archbishop, Father Bergoglio had great influence over the church's activities in Buenos Aires.

Archbishops often live in large, beautiful homes. But not Archbishop Bergoglio. In Buenos Aires, he lived in a small apartment. There were no limousines or drivers. His day started at 4:30 a.m., with two hours of prayer. To get to work, he would either take public transportation such as buses, drive his own car, or walk. In addition to the official work of the archdiocese, he personally worked with the poor, sick, and uneducated of Buenos Aires.

Archbishop Bergoglio visits a poor neighborhood in Buenos Aires in 1998.

Who's Who in the Church

Catholicism is a religion with followers around the world. The Catholic Church is divided into parishes. Members, called parishioners, attend their local church led by a pastor.

A group of parishes forms a diocese, which is headed by a bishop. A very large diocese—such as in a big city—is called an archdiocese and is led by an archbishop.

Above an archbishop is a cardinal. Most countries have one or more cardinals. The only person above a cardinal is the pope. One of a cardinal's most important duties is to elect a new pope when a pope dies.

A priest leads a mass for a parish in Uganda.

In 2001, Pope John Paul II named Archbishop Bergoglio a cardinal. With the new title, Bergoglio took a larger role in helping run the church. When the pope passed away four years later, Cardinal Bergoglio traveled to the Vatican in Rome, the headquarters of the Catholic Church. There, he voted for the next pope. Bergoglio himself received several votes, but Cardinal Joseph Ratzinger from Germany was chosen. Ratzinger became Pope Benedict XVI, the 265th pope.

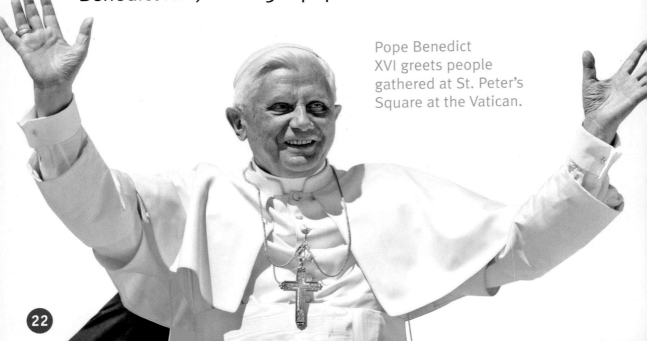

Pope Benedict XVI greets people gathered at St. Peter's Square at the Vatican.

A Sudden Turn

A pope is elected for life. But in February 2013, Pope Benedict XVI announced he was retiring. Few popes have ever done this—the last time it happened was 1415. The cardinals had to go back to the Vatican to name a new pope. The cardinals discussed the possible names they would consider. On March 13, they decided on the new pope: Cardinal Bergoglio.

Vatican City, the center of the Catholic Church, is located in Rome, but it is an independent nation-state.

Electing a Pope

When a pope dies or resigns, the Sacred College of Cardinals gathers at the Vatican. The college is made up of 120 cardinals under the age of 80. Members have a **conclave**, or private meeting, to choose the next pope. That pope is always a member of the college.

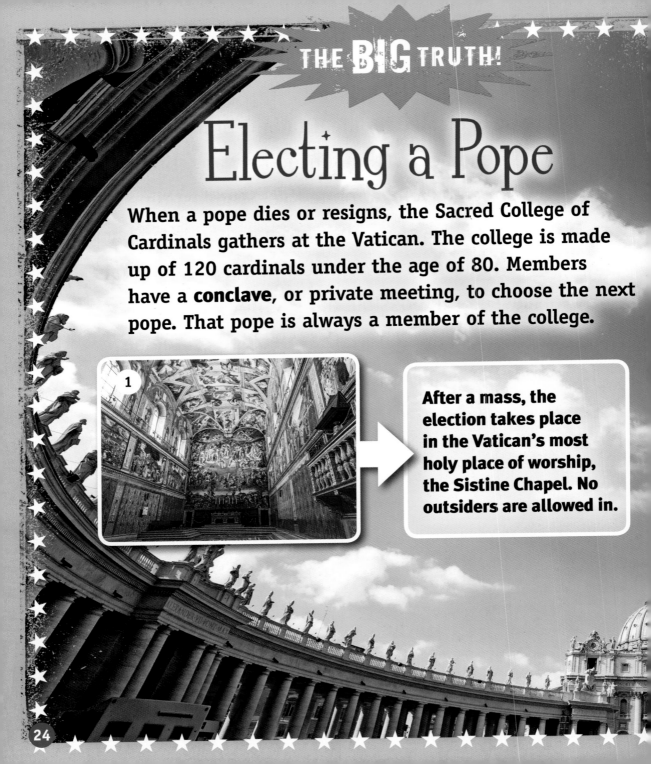

1

After a mass, the election takes place in the Vatican's most holy place of worship, the Sistine Chapel. No outsiders are allowed in.

The cardinals discuss possible new popes and cast a ballot. A person needs two-thirds of the vote plus one vote to be pope. If no one succeeds in the first ballot, the cardinals discuss further. A new ballot is cast each morning and afternoon. After three days, the cardinals take a day off for rest and prayer. If no one is selected after 30 ballots, a simple majority determines the new pope. The process can last hours or days.

After each ballot is cast, it is burned. People outside see the smoke and can tell by its color if a new pope has been chosen. The ballots are treated with chemicals. If there is no decision, the ballot produces black smoke. When a pope is selected, the smoke is white.

CHAPTER 3

Being Pope

A newly elected pope chooses the name he will be called. Bergoglio chose Pope Francis. He represents a lot of firsts: the first Jesuit pope, the first pope from the Americas, and the first pope from south of the equator. He is the first pope born outside of Europe since 741. After he was elected, Pope Francis went to greet the thousands of people who had gathered at the Vatican. He asked them one thing: "Please pray for me."

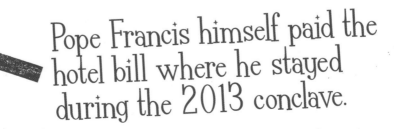

Pope Francis himself paid the hotel bill where he stayed during the 2013 conclave.

A Simple Life

Traditionally, the pope lives in fancy, beautiful rooms in the Vatican's Apostolic Palace. Pope Francis chose to move into a two-room apartment in one of the Vatican's guesthouses instead. It is simple but has everything he needs. There is no computer or smartphone. Though Pope Francis is dedicated to solving 21st-century problems, he keeps his everyday life uncomplicated.

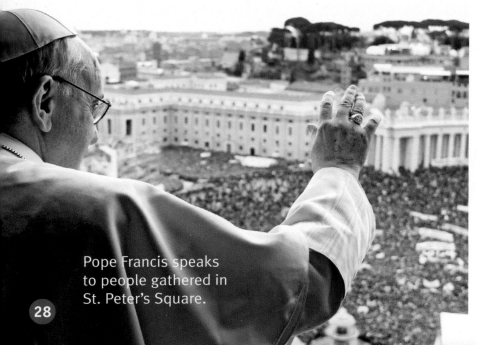

Pope Francis often eats at the Vatican cafeteria.

Pope Francis speaks to people gathered in St. Peter's Square.

Pope Francis is known to make unplanned and informal public appearances. People in Rome once met him as he stopped in a store for a pair of eyeglasses. Tourists and citizens alike often attend mass at the Vatican's local parish church, St. Anna's. Though not really part of his duties, it isn't a surprise when Pope Francis performs the service. He loves being close to the people.

The Pope's Duties

When Pope Francis arrives at his Vatican offices, it is early in the morning. He gets right to work. He meets with his advisers, discusses their projects, and plans what they will do in the future. He also works to support and improve the community where he lives. He has established homeless shelters and educational centers in the Vatican.

Timeline of the Journey to Becoming Pope

December 17, 1936

Jorge Mario Bergoglio is born.

1958

Bergoglio enters a Jesuit seminary.

1969

Bergoglio is ordained a priest.

A major part of the pope's work extends across the world. He believes that everyone on earth has a right to a home, food, and a job. Many times, he has spoken against greed and the love of money. Reaching out to governments and companies, he works toward equal opportunities for all. With this in mind, Pope Francis has helped create and support international programs that address health, poverty, and education.

1998
Bergoglio becomes the Archbishop of Buenos Aires.

2001
Pope John Paul II names Archbishop Bergoglio a cardinal.

March 13, 2013
Cardinal Bergoglio becomes Pope Francis.

Visitors to the Vatican can purchase a variety of items that feature pictures of Pope Francis.

Pope Francis has often argued that if we all work together, we can solve many problems. One of the ways he shares this message is through a papal **encyclical**. This is a letter that is sent to all the cardinals, archbishops, and bishops. They, in turn, share it with parishioners. Some encyclicals reach beyond the Catholic community to the whole world, such as Pope Francis's encyclical *Laudato Si'*, or "Praise Be to You," on the environment.

Meet and Greet

Whether at home or traveling, the pope has a packed schedule. However, he always makes time for people. Some are foreign officials on business at the Vatican. But often, he reaches out to regular people, from tourists to local residents. Thousands of people gather in St. Peter's Square at the Vatican. They wait for him to come to the window and bless them. When the pope travels, there are crowds of people hoping to see him.

Pope Francis greets crowds during his visit to Washington, D.C., in 2015.

If Pope Francis is in Rome, he holds papal audiences at the Vatican every Wednesday morning. Tickets to the audiences are free. At these events, the pope gives a small reading and a teaching, usually in Italian. The pope also makes an official appearance at the Vatican library window every Sunday at noon. But his favorite meetings are when he can talk with people, bless them, and hug them.

Pope Francis greets people as he arrives for his weekly audience.

The Popemobile

Before cars, popes used horse-drawn carriages or sedan chairs carried by official footmen. In the late 1920s, the Vatican began using cars. These vehicles were nicknamed "popemobiles." They were usually expensive luxury models with official drivers. After attempted **assassinations** on other popes in 1970 and 1981, new cars were specially designed to be highly secure. Many were open, with a clear plastic cover. The cover protected the pope while allowing people to see him. Pope Francis prefers not to use the covers, calling them "sardine cans." His favorite popemobile is a small, well-worn car he drives himself.

Pope Francis leads the
World Youth Day mass
in Brazil in 2013.

CHAPTER 4

A Man of the People

Francis took his first international trip as pope in July 2013, to Brazil. There, he celebrated World Youth Day and said mass to three million people on Rio de Janeiro's Copacabana beach. He urged people to spread their love and support to those in need. Whether they are in a poor village or from a war-torn country, he said, they are our brothers and sisters and deserve our care.

Brazil has the largest Catholic population in the world.

The pope led a mass for more than 20,000 people at Madison Square Garden in New York City in 2015.

Moving Right Along

After visiting Brazil, Pope Francis returned to the Vatican. However, he was already planning future travels. In 2014 alone, he visited Israel, Jordan, Palestine, South Korea, Albania, France, and Turkey. In 2015, he picked Sri Lanka, the Philippines, and Bosnia and Herzegovina. He also traveled to Bolivia, Ecuador, Paraguay, Cuba, and the United States. Kenya, Uganda, and the Central African Republic also saw the pope that year.

A Reunion

Everywhere the pope went, people came to greet him. In Manila, the capital of the Philippines, a record six million people attended his mass. The pope began 2016 with a brief return to Cuba before a longer visit in Mexico. This visit to Cuba was particularly historic. There, Pope Francis met with Patriarch Kirill, the head of the Russian Orthodox Church. Members of this church form the largest population within the Eastern Orthodox Church.

People display mugs and other souvenirs leading up to Pope Francis's visit to Sarajevo, Bosnia and Herzegovina, in 2015.

About 1,000 years ago, the Christian church split between the East (Orthodox) and West (Catholic). The two sides have had little to do with each other since then. Francis and Kirill are the first pope and Russian Orthodox patriarch to ever meet. The two wrote a **declaration** together. It discussed many topics, including cooperation and freedom of religion. It also talked about the struggles Christians face in some parts of the world.

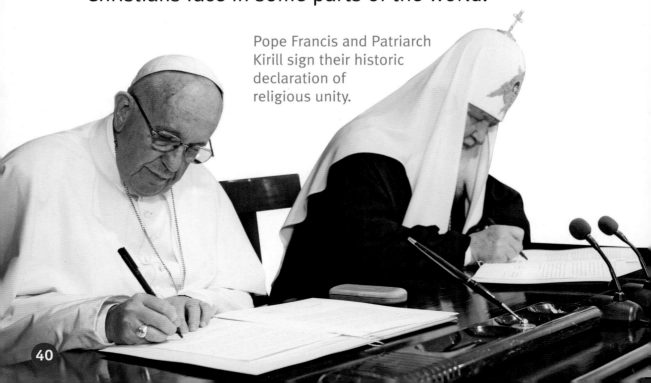

Pope Francis and Patriarch Kirill sign their historic declaration of religious unity.

Pope Francis's meetings with leaders such as President Barack Obama have had a major influence on world events.

Healing a Divide

The pope's international duties aren't limited to visits. Pope Francis has been involved in helping Cuba and the United States improve their relationship. The two nations had not officially dealt with each other for more than 50 years. In 2015, Cuba and the United States started strengthening their ties.

Pope Francis poses for a selfie at the Vatican in 2014.

Joy Around the World

Pope Francis is known for his charm and for going "off script." Though his speeches are always written ahead of time, he often says more than planned. He also frequently stops to take selfies or bless someone. He has traded hats with people and laughed over jokes with them. Sometimes, the pope's followers surprise him, too. More than once, Pope Francis has met a child dressed to look like him, and it made him laugh.

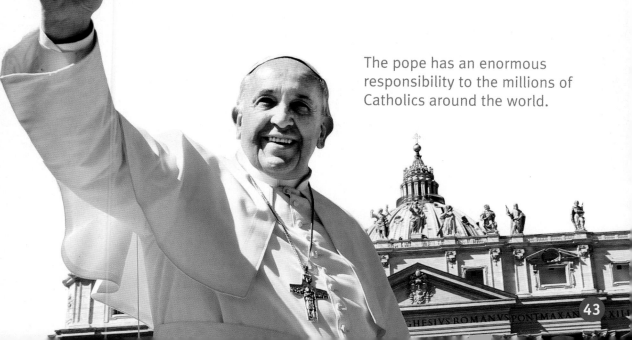

Wherever he goes, Pope Francis spreads a message of love and humility. He does this with words in his writings and speeches. He also demonstrates these qualities in his actions, from blessing people in prison to taking the bus instead of an expensive private car. The pope never forgets the challenge of leading and serving the entire Catholic community. With this in mind, he often reminds his followers: "Pray for me." ★

The pope has an enormous responsibility to the millions of Catholics around the world.

Number of Catholics around the world, as of 2016: About 1.27 billion

Number of Jesuits around the world, as of 2016: About 17,000

Time it takes to become a priest in the Society of Jesus: 11 years, sometimes more

Age of Pope Francis at election: 76

Number of followers the pope has on Twitter: More than 4 million

Number of languages Pope Francis speaks: 4— Spanish, German, Italian, and English

Largest gathering in history of human beings for any reason: More than 6 million people, January 18, 2015, in the Philippines, for a mass given by Pope Francis

Did you find the truth?

F Pope Francis was born in Italy.

T Pope Francis taught in schools for many years.

Resources

Books

Francis, Pope. *Dear Pope Francis: The Pope Answers Letters From Children Around the World*. Chicago: Loyola Press, 2016.

Kramer, Barbara. *Pope Francis*. Washington, D.C.: National Geographic, 2015.

Monge, Marlyn, and Jaymie Stuart Wolfe. *Jorge From Argentina: The Story of Pope Francis for Children*. Boston: Pauline Books & Media, 2013.

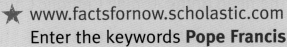

Visit this Scholastic Web site for more information on Pope Francis:
★ www.factsfornow.scholastic.com
Enter the keywords **Pope Francis**

Important Words

assassinations (uh-sas-uh-NAY-shuhnz) murders of people who are well-known or important

ballot (BAL-uht) a way of voting secretly, using a machine or slips of paper

conclave (KAHN-klayv) a private or secret meeting

declaration (dek-luh-RAY-shuhn) an announcement, especially an official one

encyclical (in-SIH-klih-kul) a letter or announcement to all the members of a group

novice (NAH-vis) a new member of a religious group who is preparing to become a monk, nun, or priest

ordained (or-DAYND) officially made a minister, priest, rabbi, or other religious authority

orders (OR-durz) groups within a religious community that follow particular methods of worship or service

pope (POPE) the head of the Roman Catholic Church

seminary (SEM-uh-ner-ee) a school that trains students to become priests, ministers, or rabbis

theology (thee-AH-luh-jee) the study of religion and religious beliefs

Index

Page numbers in **bold** indicate illustrations.

About the Author

Marie Morreale is the author of many biographies. She attended New York University as an English/creative writing major and began her writing and editorial career in New York City. As the editor of teen/music magazines *Teen Machine* and *Jam!*, she covered TV, film, and music personalities and interviewed superstars such as Michael Jackson, Britney Spears, and Justin Timberlake/*NSYNC. Morreale also worked as an editor and writer at Little Golden Books.

Today, she is the executive editor, media, of Scholastic Classroom Magazines and writes about pop culture, sports, news, and special events. Morreale lives in New York City and is entertained daily by her two Maine coon cats, Cher and Sullivan.